THE ORIGINAL

Rubaiyyat
of Omar Khayaam

A NEW TRANSLATION
WITH CRITICAL COMMENTARIES
BY
Robert Graves
AND
Omar Ali-Shah

OMEN PRESS, INC.
TUCSON, ARIZONA
1972

First Paperback Printing, 1972

*Published by arrangement with
Doubleday & Company, Inc.*

ISBN 0-912358-38-6

The Original Rubaiyyat of Omar Khayaam

The Original Rubaiyyat of Omar Khayaam

CONTENTS

The Fitz-Omar Cult by Robert Graves   1

Historical Preface by Omar Ali-Shah   32

The Rubaiyyat   47

Notes on the Translation   77

Two Comparative Renderings   82

Select Bibliography of Manuscripts   84

THE FITZ-OMAR CULT

ROBERT GRAVES

Most lifelong admirers of Edward Fitzgerald's translation—
or, to borrow his own jocular word, 'transmogrification'—
of Omar Khayaam's *Rubaiyyat* are unaware that the fifteenth-
century manuscript at Oxford from which he supposedly
worked is far from being 'perhaps the earliest in existence'.
And those few who know of the supposedly thirteenth-
century manuscript now at Cambridge and translated by
Professor Arberry in 1952 may be loth to believe that an
authoritative twelfth-century text has been available to Sufic
students in Afghanistan since shortly after Khayaam's death
more than eight hundred years ago.

I have made an English verse translation of this earliest
and most authoritative *Rubaiyyat* at the request and under
the surveillance of Omar Ali-Shah, the Sufi poet and
classical Persian scholar, to whose family the manuscript
belongs. Although he had recently published his own
excellent French rendering, in prose and verse, of another
early Sufic manuscript, Saadi's *Garden of the Rose*, Omar
Ali-Shah now contented himself with a literal and annotated
'crib' of the *Rubaiyyat* for my faithful recasting in the nearest
possible approach to poetry. To be entrusted with this task
was the greatest poetic compliment that I had ever been paid;
nor can I remember having been so moved by any ancient
poem since Edwardian days when I first came across the *Iliad*
at my public school.

Robert Pace records in his *De Fructu* (1517) that an old English parish priest was once corrected by his ecclesiastical superior for reading the Latin text of the Mass—*quod in ore sumpsimus* ('which we have taken by mouth') as *quod in ore mumpsimus*; a nonsensical misspelling found in his familiar battered missal. The priest protested indignantly: 'I will not change my old *mumpsimus* for your new *sumpsimus*.' King Henry VIII referred to this in his 1550 Parliamentary speech with: 'Some be too stiff in their old *mumpsimus*; others too busy and curious in their new *sumpsimus*.' Nevertheless, King Henry, for all his breach with the Papacy, knew which was the better reading.

Edward Fitzgerald (1809–1883) is widely celebrated as the supposed originator of the *Rubaiyyat*, rather than as an easygoing amateur Orientalist who constructed a mid-Victorian poem of his own from an ill-understood classical Persian text. Its publication in 1858 coincided with a strong anti-devotional movement among young English ex-Protestants encouraged in their revolt by Charles Darwin's newly broached doctrine of Evolution. As a result, Fitzgerald's *Rubaiyyat* became suddenly famous and is now, for its length, the most frequent source of modern entries in English Dictionaries of Familiar Quotations, and a true *mumpsimus*. For four generations, indeed, by an evil paradox, Omar Khayaam's mystical poem has been erroneously accepted throughout the West as a drunkard's rambling profession of the hedonistic creed: 'let us eat and drink for tomorrow we die.' Khayaam is also credited with a flat denial either that life has any ultimate sense or purpose, or that the Creator can be, in justice, allowed any of the mercy, wisdom or perfection illogically attributed to Him; which is precisely the opposite view to that expressed in Khayaam's original.

Not many years after the Norman Conquest of England, this middle-aged Persian University professor broke away from his academic colleagues at the College of Nishapur and returned to the Sufic way of thought from which, perhaps because obvious recourse to it might have prejudiced his formal education, he appears to have lapsed in early manhood. He was at that time not only a famous orthodox Moslem philosopher, but also an inventive mathematician whose treatise on algebra is still highly regarded, and an out-standing astronomer. He had also played an important part in reforming the Moslem calendar, some five centuries before the Christian calendar was similarly taken in hand. This change of heart caused a scandal. His University colleagues felt only scorn for Sufis, whom they regarded at the best as heretical enthusiasts; yet now their revered colleague had started writing ecstatic poetry and placed himself in pupilage once more to a Sheikh, or teacher, who would treat him like a school-boy throughout the customary twelve years of Sufic training! Khayaam would even be expected to ask this Sheikh not merely for permission to write poems but for suggestions on the subjects and the metre. It will, in fact, have been the Sheikh who gave him Wine as a subject for poetic meditation, rather than Oil, Bread or Figs, all of which had mystical Sufic meanings attached to them.

In Khayaam's stanza 70 we find a reference to this Sheikh,

who advised him to think with his heart and not be influenced
by literary or theological tradition:

> But prudently my Teacher warned me: 'Pen
> And Tablet, Heaven and Hell, lie in yourself.'

Khayaam treats wine in Sufic fashion as a metaphor of the
ecstasy excited by divine love: a simple concept not readily
grasped by Westerners, if only because they are convinced
that wine-drinking was forbidden by Mohammed in the
Koran. This is a mistake: only the drinking of date-liquor,
which caused a great deal of bloodshed and disorder in
seventh-century Arabia, came under the Prophet's ban.
Wine had long been used for religious purposes by the
Hebrews (many of whose doctrines Mohammed accepted)
especially at their Feast of Tabernacles. Because of the divine-
love metaphor attached to wine, four cups had also been
compulsory at the First Corn Festival of Passover, which
commemorated both God's gift of bread to man and His
rescue of Israel from Egyptian bondage. Hence the appearance
of wine in the Last Supper Gospel narrative, from St Paul's
account of which in *I Corinthians XI*, 23, the Christian
communion rite was formalized. Nevertheless, puritanical
theologians of Khayaam's day had attempted to put a *syeg*,
or hedge, around the use of date-liquor by banning all other
intoxicants: as Orthodox Jewish rabbis still keep a *syeg* around
breaches of the Fourth Commandment by forbidding even
the poking of a fire on the Sabbath day. The Sufic wine
metaphor will have been borrowed either from the Hebrew
Scriptures or from a common source, perhaps Philistine; 'wine'

in Greek, Hebrew, Arabic and Persian being a loan-word from Minoan, and the Philistines having originated in Crete.

Hooke in his *Myth and Ritual*, Patai in his *Man and Temple*, and other Biblical historians hold that the vintage festival of Tabernacles commemorated a former Divine Marriage between Jehovah's royal or priestly representative and a virgin chosen to represent 'Matrona', the female personification of Israel. The 'booths' or 'tabernacles' seem to have been lesser bridal chambers, built in sympathetic imitation of the Sacred Chamber, namely the Holy of Holies, where the two cherubim carved above the Mercy Seat of the Ark were, according to Talmudic tradition (*B. Yoma 54a*), bound in a close embrace—'even as a man embraces his bride'. This divine marriage, which had been performed for centuries in Babylon and many other Middle-Eastern cities, was discontinued at Jerusalem after the destruction of the first Temple. Yet the Feast of Tabernacles continued to be celebrated and the divine-marriage tradition of the *Song of Solomon*—King Solomon whose bride was a virgin from Shunem—survived in its chanting at all Jewish weddings, where the bridegroom was treated as a King, and the bride as his Queen.

Numerous verses in the *Song of Solomon* convey this sense:

I, 2   Let me kiss thee with the kisses of my mouth
For thy love is better than wine. . . .
I, 4   We will be glad and rejoice in Thee.
We will remember Thy love more than wine. The upright love Thee.

II, 1   I am the rose of Sharon and the lily of the
Valley.

*[Tristram reports that the Arab peasantry use 'lily' for
any brilliantly coloured flower at all resembling a lily,
such as tulip, anemone or ranunculus. See Khayaam's
stanzas 19 and 42.]*

II,
4–5   He brought me to his banqueting house and his
banner over me was love. Stay me with flagons,
comfort me with apples, for I am sick of love.

*[i.e. 'love sick' . . . Apple wine is often mentioned in the
Jewish Mishna. It was made from Cydonian apples:
i.e. quinces. Apples did not grow in Palestine. In Greece
the quince was consecrated to the Love Goddess.]*

VIII,
9   The roof of thy mouth is like the best wine
for my beloved, that goeth down sweetly,
causing the lips of the ancient ones to speak . . .

VIII,
2   I would lead thee and bring thee into my
mother's house, who would instruct me.
I would cause thee to drink of spiced wine
of the juice of my pomegranate.

VIII,
11–12   Solomon had a vineyard at Baal-Shamon: he let
out the vineyard unto keepers, everyone for the
fruit thereof was to bring a thousand pieces of
silver.
My vineyard which is mine is before me. Thou,
O Solomon, must have a thousand, and those
that keep the fruit thereof two hundred.

The Pharisees glossed this poem, since they could not easily suppress it, as a dramatic exposition of God's love for Israel, and of Israel's for God: and so they also explained the Cherubim's embrace.

Later, the Christians followed suit. The following chapter-glosses are found in the King James English Bible:

The Church's love unto Christ . . .
He showeth His love for her and giveth gracious promise . . .
The Church, having a taste of Christ's love, is sick of love . . .
The love of the Church of Christ . . . The vehemency of love . . . The Church prayeth for Christ's coming.

The Sufis accepted this divine-love metaphor; but because Mohammedan women were kept in far closer subjection than the Jewish, whose 'levity' at the Feast of Tabernacles gave the Pharisees constant anxiety, and because the Matrona tradition was Hebrew, not Arabian or Persian, a rapt brotherly love of fellow-initiates was substituted by the Sufis for erotic love.

Every sacrifice at the Jerusalem Temple was accompanied by a libation of unmixed wine to Jehovah. And we find several praises of wine in the Old Testament, although Rechabites, Nazarites and Prophets were forbidden to touch it and Temple priests also had to abstain while on duty:

Psalm CIV, 15	Wine maketh glad the heart of man.
Proverbs XXXI, 6–7	Give strong drink unto him that is ready to perish, and wine unto those that be of

heavy hearts. Let him drink and forget
his poverty and remember his misery no
more.

Judges IX,
12–13 Then said the trees to the Vine: 'Come
and rule over us.' And the Vine said unto
them: 'Should I leave my wine, which
cheereth God and man, to be promoted
over all trees?'

On the other hand, drunkenness is frequently used by the
abstemious Hebrew prophets as a metaphor not of religious
ecstasy but of irreligious folly: *Isaiah LI,* 17ff, *Jeremiah XXV,*
15ff, *Ezekiel XXIII,* 33 etc. Thus the Nishapur puritans could
justify their un-Koranic ban on wine as being traditional and
also as serving to preserve Law and Order. Khayaam, however,
rejected this view, while also rejecting (stanza 13) the
equally un-Koranic doctrine, used by Moslem chieftains to
encourage their soldiers, that to die in battle would take a
man directly to a Paradisal drinking-bower inexhaustibly
stocked with wine and attended by bevies of luscious houris.

A fugitive stanza of Omar Khayaam's, quoted by Omar
Ali-Shah's elder brother, Idries, in his book *The Sufis,* runs:

> Without the taste of wine, my life is lost;
> A generous draught alone holds me upright.
> The Saki's voice enslaves me: how I sigh for
> That 'One cup more' for which I cannot reach!

Idries Shah authoritatively glosses this as referring to the
condition reached by a Sufi when his ecstatic experience—a

figurative drunkenness—reveals a hidden dimension beyond his normal habit of thought.

Edward Fitzgerald first met the *Rubaiyyat* through Edward Cowell, a fellow-undergraduate at Trinity College, Cambridge. Cowell was a fair Persian scholar, for those times, and, according to an anonymous biographical preface attached to several modern editions of Fitzgerald's work,

> 'may be said to have disentombed Omar's poems from oblivion, since labouring as they did under the original sin of heresy and atheism they were seldom looked at. Omar was no more of a Mohammedan than many of our best writers are Christians.'

Much the same criticism was once made of the mystical poems written by a sixteenth-century Spaniard, Juan de la Cruz (John of the Cross) who, coming under Sufic influences by way of Ramón Llull, used the same wine metaphor in his celebration of Divine Love, though his poems were more directly based on the *Song of Solomon* than Khayaam's. But Juan de la Cruz was eventually canonized; and Khayaam's famous contemporary, Abu Mohammed al-Ghazali, having triumphantly vindicated the 'philosophic' teaching of the Koran by close logical argument, won general respect for the Sufic point of view both inside and outside Islam. Moreover, the senior male line in descent from the Prophet himself had transmitted, and still transmits, to its sons the secret Sufic doctrine that he is recorded to have bequeathed them; so that to call Khayaam 'no more of a Mohammedan than many of the best English writers are Christians' borders on the absurd.

Fitzgerald, justifying his earlier free translations from Calderón's Spanish and from Aeschylus's Greek, wrote:

> 'in the absence of a poet who can recreate in his own language the body and soul of a foreign poet, the best translator is one who paraphrases the original work while conserving the author's spirit.'

'A sort of literary metempsychosis,' agreed George Saintsbury, the most influential critic of the early twentieth century and a fervent admirer of Fitzgerald's *Rubaiyyat*. He wrote in his preface to one edition: 'This is a *chose jugée*: depreciation of it would be idle paradox; praise is superfluous'—believing, like almost everyone else, that Fitzgerald had magisterially imposed decent literary order on a jumbled ragbag of discarded Oriental verse. He commented also:

> 'Omar Khayaam's *Rubaiyyat* is a collection of some eight hundred and odd quatrains, genuine and doubtful, dealing with subjects extremely difficult to label or ticket under one head . . . Whether we have ever had a greater translator than Fitzgerald, whether we have ever had one nearly so great, remains a question. What is quite certain is that we have never had anyone who, in verse, confining himself almost, if not quite, wholly to translation . . . did it so magnificently. In all his translated work—the bulk of it from Greek and Spanish—he has given himself the widest licence of paraphrase, omission and addition. Whether he has gone wider still in part of his other Persian borrowings—his *Salaman and Absal*—

I am not in a position to say, for I do not know Persian. And I should perhaps be allowed to add that his original dialogue *Euphranor* and his "collected" *Polonius* hardly deserve to be called first-rate. On the other hand to us, legitimately, Fitzgerald *is* Omar Khayaam and one may almost dare to say Omar Khayaam *is* Fitzgerald . . . It is impossible not to smile and difficult not to laugh, when one finds a faithful and admiring friend like Professor Cowell, who himself was in a way one of the begetters of this masterpiece, looking in vain for the original of one of Fitz's lines, and writing to him about it in vain from Calcutta; but finding with a sort of resignation that the author never cared to alter it!'

Does depreciation of his work still seem idle paradox? And how could a man like Fitzgerald who was incapable, as Saintsbury confesses, of writing first-class original work, recreate that of so extraordinary a predecessor? In fact, being no poet himself, Saintsbury was blind to Fitzgerald's obvious shortcomings in the verse craftsmanship on which his fame chiefly depends. Fitzgerald's basic mistake had been to choose a verse form difficult enough to handle in an original poem and almost impossible to use in translation: namely a strict decasyllabic iambic quatrain with three rhyming lines and one unrhymed. Not only are the chances extremely remote of finding three rhymes in English which will exactly match the sense of the Persian verse, but an unvaried sequence of iambics tires the alertest ear.

Take stanza 50 in Fitzgerald's second version as an instance of his failure, even when disfiguring the sense, to write a convincingly simple quatrain:

> The Ball no Question makes of Ayes and Noes
> But right or left as strikes the Player goes.
> And He that toss'd thee down into the Field
> He knows about it all, He knows—He knows.

'The Ball no Question makes' is a clumsy inversion of sense order, inappropriately based on Latin poetic practice, like his:

> I sometimes think that never blows so red
> The Rose as where some buried Caesar bled.

Here (stanza 24) the rhyme *red* dictates the inversion, and 'I sometimes think' does not match the original direct statement (our 19):

> Each rose or tulip bed that you encounter
> Is sure to mark a king's last resting-place.

Nor, by the way, were the Persians interested, as Fitzgerald pretends, in the sepulchres of Roman Caesars. The Emperor Valerian whom they defeated and captured at Edessa in A.D. 260 was, historians say, 'subjected to every possible ignominy that Oriental cruelty could devise, and granted no grave when he succumbed to prolonged ill-treatment; for his skin was then stuffed and preserved in the largest national Temple.' Nor do *buried* Caesars bleed: the Emperor Julian, mortally wounded by a Persian arrow in A.D. 363, was interred by his officers only when dead.

In Fitzgerald's stanza 50 (second version), again, the line:

But right or left as strikes the Player goes

is a no less clumsy inversion than 'no Question makes of Ayes and Noes': it might well mean 'as a bright idea strikes the player', rather than 'as the player strikes the ball.' And not only could 'Ayes and Noes'—a jocular Parliamentary metaphor irrelevant to the polo-field—be mistaken in recitation for 'Eyes and Nose' but it rhymes illegitimately (except as a Chaucerian 'French rhyme') with 'He knows'. The original Khayaam stanza (74) runs:

Poor ball, struck by Fate's heavy polo-mallet,
Running whichever way it drives you, numbed
Of sense, though He who set you on your course,
He knows, He knows, He knows.

Why Fitzgerald has suppressed Omar's polo metaphor is hard to answer: perhaps he feared it would be unintelligible to the English, who did not take up polo until the 1860s. At any rate, his line:

And He that toss'd thee down into the Field

drags, because of an unnecessary 'into' which does not occur in the original. Too many of Fitzgerald's stanzas lack the controlled tenseness required for a religious poem; and few can escape detailed criticism of their slipshod sense, faulty grammatic construction and neo-romantic affectation. The extent of the liberties that he took in translation can be conveniently shown by comparing Khayaam's stanza 64 with stanza 42 in Fitzgerald's Second Edition, which runs:

> And lately, by the Tavern Door agape,
> Came shining through the Dusk an Angel shape
> Bearing a Vessel on his Shoulder; and
> He bid me taste of it; and 'twas the grape.

Khayaam had written ironically:

> In drink this evening, as I passed the tavern,
> A fellow toper met me with a flask.
> Cried I: 'Old man, have you no awe of God?'
> 'Comé,' he said, 'God is bountiful. Come, drink!'

Fitzgerald's famous 'Thou beside me singing in the Wilderness' has been the subject of countless Burne-Jonesian illustrations since Fitzgerald first published it; and 'Thou' is always depicted as a handsome young houri. In Khayaam's original (11 and 12), however, the 'Thou' does not sing, and is not a houri but merely his Sufi fellow-initiate with whom he meditates over a book of poems.

Fitzgerald was Irish on both sides of his family: his father, a Kilkenny Purcell, having married a Waterford Fitzgerald and added her name to his. What attracted Edward Fitzgerald to Persian poetry is said to have been his erroneous belief that *Erin* and *Iran* were etymologically connected; yet he turned his back on Ireland and its poetic tradition, was educated at Cambridge University, and lived all the rest of his life as an English gentleman at Woodbridge in Suffolk. Private means made a literary dilettante of him, and he cultivated among others the friendship of such eminent Victorians as Tennyson and Thackeray. In November, 1832, at the age of twenty-three, he wrote:

> I am of that superior race of men that are quite content to hear themselves talk and read their own writings.

and in 1846, at the age of thirty-seven:

> I have been all my life apprenticed to this heavy business of idleness; and am not yet master of my craft; the gods are too just to suffer that I should.

Idleness did not, however, draw him into laziness or fashionable debauch, or on to the Turf. He chose for his favourite motto: 'Plain living and high thinking', and was generally agreed to be 'a gentleman with a kindly and whimsical philosophy, who did nobody any harm'—not even his wife, a Quaker, whom he married briefly and soon discarded:

> 'With all the overflowing amiability of his nature there were mingled certain peculiarities, or waywardnesses, which were more suitable to the freedom of celibacy than to the staidness of matrimonial life. A separation took place by mutual consent and Fitzgerald behaved with the generosity and unselfishness which were apparent in all his whims no less than in his deliberate actions.'

According to George Saintsbury, the immediate cause of the separation was that he could not bear the rustle of his bride's silk skirts; in fact he rated any sort of female companionship far lower than brief coastal yacht-cruises from Lowestoft with an intimate friend, a couple of sailors, a large pasty, a few books and a generous supply of wine. The sea meant so much to Fitzgerald that, because Khayaam, a landsman living a week's travel away from the nearest sea (and a tideless one at that), had not referred to it in the *Rubaiyyat*, he supplied this lack with an intrusive purple patch of his own (36):

> Earth could not answer; nor the Seas that mourn
> In flowing purple, of their Lord forlorn;
> Nor Heaven with those eternal Signs reveal'd
> And hidden by the sleeve of Night and Morn.

Which Lord, by the way? None has been mentioned. And have Night and Morn only a single sleeve between them?

Such was the man who chose Omar Khayaam to provide him with his literary metempsychosis, yet who, as we read in another biographical preface:

> 'dealt with the *Rubaiyyat* as though he had the licence of absolute authorship, changing, transforming and manipulating the substance of the Persian quatrains with singular freedom'.

Heron-Allen who has made a careful analysis of Fitzgerald's sources, finds that he incorporated borrowings from Attar, Hafiz, Saadi and Jami—all, as it happens, Persian Sufis—in his transmogrification of the *Rubaiyyat*. After being taken up enthusiastically by Swinburne, Dante Gabriel Rossetti, Meredith, Sir Richard Burton, and a crowd of lesser writers,

Fitzgerald published five different versions of his composition before his death in 1883. The vogue of 'Old Omar' soon spread to America:

> 'where readers who caught the infection were in the habit of buying up numerous copies of the book for gratuitous distribution; and where the fortuitous meeting of two strangers who were Omar-lovers immediately established a close bond of friendship.'

Fitzgerald writes in stanza 55 (Second Edition)—but the first two lines are clumsy to the point of unintelligibility:

> The Vine had struck a Fibre which about
> If clings my Being—let the Sufi flout;
> Of my Base metal may be filed a key
> That shall unlock the Door he howls without.

In Khayaam's original stanza (79) neither vine nor fibre, nor base metal, nor door, nor Sufi occurs:

> But while the Eternal One created me
> He word by word spelt out my lesson, love,
> And seized my heart and from a fragment cut
> Keys to the storehouse of Reality.

The 'struck Fibre of the Vine' in Fitzgerald's version is lifted from another Persian poet; and the inclusion of anti-Sufi propaganda seems in part due to pique against a rival translator, M. Nicolas, the French Consul at Resht. M. Nicolas had published a literal translation into French of the

Rubaiyyat from a Teheran text, and annotated it in the Sufic
sense under the guidance of a Persian sheikh: pointing out,
for instance, where 'Saki' means 'God' and where 'wine'
means 'love'. This book appeared in 1867 while Fitzgerald
was busy on his Second Edition; and with Professor Cowell's
support he devoted some pages of its foreword to refuting
Nicolas's theory that Omar had 'given himself with passion
to the study of Sufic philosophy'. He added that two at least
of the 468 verses contained in the Teheran collection were
directed against the Sufis and could not be regarded as
interpolations.

Khayaam may well have privately mocked at the 'painted'
or false Sufis, very much as Jesus denounced the 'painted'
Pharisees (translated as 'hypocrites' in the King James
version of the Gospels) while enjoining his disciples
(*Matthew XXIII*, 1) to observe all the rules for moral behaviour
laid down by the reputable Pharisees of the School of Hillel
who ruled the Sanhedrin under its President Gamaliel. Nor
will even the most literal-minded Western puritan deny that
when Jesus is reported as saying: 'I will drink no more of
this fruit of the vine until I drink it new in the Kingdom of
Heaven,' he was speaking in metaphor. After all, the
Communion cup is securely established in Church doctrine
as a symbol of divine love between God and man.

Perhaps, also, Fitzgerald's literal view of Khayaam's
drunkenness reflects regret for having as a young man
toyed with seventeenth-century mysticism. He had now, at
any rate, been reassured by his vacillating and equally ill-
informed friend, Cowell, that

'though the Sultan showered favours on Omar, his
Epicurean audacity of thought and speech caused him to
be regarded askance in his own Time and Country . . .
He is said to have been especially hated and dreaded by
the Sufis, whose Practice he ridiculed and whose Faith
amounted to little more than his own, when stript of
the Mysticism and formal recognition of Islamism
under which Omar would not hide.'

So Fitzgerald invites his readers to

'believe with me that, while the Wine that Omar
celebrates is simply the juice of the grape, he bragged
more than he drank, in very defiance perhaps of that
Spiritual wine which left its Votaries sunk in Hypocrisy
and Disgust.'

He has suppressed the last of Khayaam's three most explicit
stanzas (25, 26, 27) (24, 25 in Fitzgerald's Second Edition) which
define his position as a Sufi. He has also mistranslated
Khayaam's first two, as follows:

Alike for those who for Today prepare
And those that after a Tomorrow stare,
A Muezzin from the Tower of Darkness cries:
'Fools, your Reward is neither Here nor There!'

Why, all the Saints and Sages who discuss'd
Of the Two Worlds so learnedly, are thrust
Like Foolish Prophets forth; their words to Scorn
Are scattered, and their Mouths are stopped with Dust.

The Muezzin, with his talk of rewards, is Fitzgerald's own creation. The original runs:

> Some ponder long on doctrine and belief,
> Some teeter between certitude and doubt.
> Suddenly out of hiding leaps the Guide
> With: 'Fools, the Way is neither that nor this.'
>
> Most of them, gone before we go, my Saki,
> Drowse in their dusty bed of pride, my Saki.
> Drink yet again and hear the truth at last:
> 'Whatever words they spoke were wind, my Saki.'
>
> Yet those who proved most perfect of our kind
> Mounted the soaring Burak of their thoughts.
> Study your essence: like the Firmament
> Your head will turn and turn, vertiginously.

This last stanza is written in honour of Khayaam's Sufi teachers, and its second half directs his reader's attention to the sacred whirling Dervish dance. This dance has the same physical intent as the baskets in which certain oracular Greek Sibyls, including the Cumaean one, were swung around until they were giddy: namely, to empty the mind of all irrelevant circumstantial thought, and so prepare it for divine communication.

Some verses in the *Rubaiyyat* have been read by uninformed readers as heretical and even blasphemous, largely because one of Khayaam's favourite methods, borrowed from other Sufi poets, such as his elder contemporary, the blind Abu

el-Ali el-Maari, was to imitate and follow up a false line of
thought in order to demonstrate its shallowness. Jesus had
used much the same method in his parable of the Unjust
Steward (*Luke XVI*, 1–12) ending up with the satiric command
to make friends with the Mammon of Unrighteousness and
buy one's way into Heaven with it—a command which a
great body of Christians have taken seriously. One must
therefore expect instances of dramatic mimicry, sometimes
of his orthodox theological colleagues, sometimes of the
uneducated, sometimes of real drunkards; sometimes, doubtless, of his own unredeemed self.

It should be remembered, too, that in Khayaam's day, the
authorship even of a poem that won general acceptance was
held to be its own reward, nor were any copyright laws in
force. Throughout the world, of course, true poets neither
compete with one another in fame, nor feel much concern
for the commercial success of their work. Therefore to assess
the poetic debt that Khayaam owed to el-Maari's *Luzum* or
that St. John of the Cross owed perhaps to the *Rubaiyyat*,
and certainly to *The Song of Solomon*, is irrelevant in the context
of mysticism, however interesting the literary historians
may find it.

The Sufis held, and hold, that poets should discourage
personality cults: and there is much to say for this view.
Certainly the semi-divine glory later attached to such names
as Virgil, Dante, Milton and Goethe has long tempted young
poets to aim at comparable literary eminence instead of
simply being themselves. Nevertheless, the Sufis' neglect
even to fix a canon of Omar Khayaam's poems—some of the

truest and sharpest of the fugitive ones belong with the *Rubaiyyat*—has its disadvantages. True poems are far more than moralistic texts, because they possess a compelling rhythm and diction, no less idiosyncratic than the poet's hand-writing, which uninspired moralistic verse lacks. Besides, any poet who lives in an otherwise barren period is reduced by loneliness to communing with poets long dead. It is difficult for English poets to evoke the comradely presence of Mr. Anon, whose Border ballads are by now so worn down and altered by folk-singers that their personal flavour has long been adulterated or lost.

The original one hundred and eleven stanzas of the *Rubaiyyat* were, as Fitzgerald notes, enlarged by later accretions to several hundred, some of them containing what M. Nicolas termed 'revolting sensualities which I refrain from translating'. The fifteenth-century Bodleian manuscript said to have been consulted by Fitzgerald—comparison of the various MSS, by the way, does not bear this out, and I am puzzled by the discrepancy—contains 158 stanzas. Yet few Sufis protest against this muddying of the waters. They merely distinguish false thought from true; aware that the same poet may have presented both in the course of his career. They are right on the whole: popular adoration of Shakespeare, for instance, has made even his shabbiest work sacrosanct.

Fitzgerald's additions to the Khayaam corpus seem falser than any. It could, of course, be pleaded that ancient custom— and Fitzgerald, despite his 'waywardnesses', was rooted in custom and entertained a particular respect for the Laws of

England—has never prevented anonymous writers from fathering their own works on admired ancients. Immediate instances are the *Books of Moses,* the *Proverbs of Solomon,* the *Psalms of David,* the *Hymns of Homer.* And it is to Fitzgerald's credit that the First Edition of his 'transmogrification'—the two hundred copies published by Messrs. Quaritch which, after proving unsaleable at five shillings each, were marked down to one penny and then found speculative and satisfied buyers—did not bear his own name on the title page. Later, of course, he fell from grace and accepted the 'Fitz-Omar' cult without demur.

He has been applauded for imposing his own structure of thought on the *Rubaiyyat,* on the supposed ground that none was to be found in the original. Yet it needed no Sufi to recognize the *Rubaiyyat's* temporal pattern from dawn to dead of night, from youth to old age; its central verses recording the metaphysical noontide torments of a passionate mind. Fitzgerald dared to use Khayaam's awesome culminating stanza as no. 20 in his own First Edition, while suppressing it in his Second; and placed Khayaam's no. 7, which describes the early rose-season of life, as no. 102 in his First Edition, and as no. 70 in his Second.

Among Khayaam's accusations by later Moslem critics has been his alleged unKoranic belief in transmigration of souls; they seem to have misconstrued his metaphor of cresses and violets spontaneously growing from the graves of beautiful girls, and tulips from those of kings. Yet that these are mere metaphors is shown by the suggestion that his own dead clay could be moulded into a jug. He knew, of course, that corpses do not return to the clay from which God is said to have moulded man, but corrupt and turn into dust. What he meant was that the power resident in his poems would, he hoped, continue to pour out the wine of love for Sufic successors; as do traditional memories of beautiful women or noble kings.

An anecdote quoted by Professor Browne in his *Literary History of Persia* as an argument for Omar's belief in transmigration of souls can similarly be explained away.

> 'Omar was about to pass the gate of his old college at Nishapur when a string of donkeys loaded with bricks for the repair of its walls entered it. One donkey, however, baulked and would not follow the rest. Omar smilingly went up to it and extemporized the verse:
>
> > *Since you resigned your post, a name*
> > *Is missing from the Roll, old friend;*
> > *Your nails bunch into hooves; for shame—*
> > *Your beard now hangs from the wrong end!*
>
> Omar's Sufi disciples, watching the ass now obediently enter the college grounds, asked: "Wise man, what does this mean?" Omar answered: "The ass's soul once belonged to a professor at this college. It was reluctant to enter while in its present shameful form, and consented only when recognized by a former colleague."'

Like most Sufic anecdotes, this has a multiple meaning. Khayaam's former colleagues had, it seems, called him an ass for resigning his Chair; he was now insisting that he would indeed be an ass if he decided to return. At the same time he was showing that gentle words addressed to an unruly beast of burden can resign it to its lot; also suggesting that the doctrine of metempsychosis—held by Indians who believed that a morally degraded man would be punished in his next incarnation by a physical degradation in the scale of living things—made better metaphorical than literal sense.

Fitzgerald argues against the probability of Khayaam's having used wine to symbolize divine love, by asking two questions: 'If the wine were spiritual, how could one wash the body with it when dead?' And 'why make cups of its dead clay to be filled with *La Divinité* by some succeeding mystic?' These questions can be readily answered. The first metaphor refers to the use of wine as a disinfectant—as in the parable of the Good Samaritan (*Luke X*, 34). Khayaam is in fact pleading that, when he dies, his friends will wash him in wine, that is to say will remember only the best of him, so that the wine's bouquet will scent the air above his grave (100) and make passing topers sniff and find themselves 'ignobly' drunk. This amounts to a plea for keeping his memory fresh in a collection of love-poems to enchant unacademic readers with the same capacity for love as himself—'ignobly' is, of course, a sarcasm. He has strengthened the metaphor by mentioning cups of wine formed from his dead clay, as in the case of the lover (96) whose clay became a wine jug. He also makes a mocking confession (101) that he besmirched his purity, after he took to prayer and fasting, by an illicit sip of wine: that is to say by renouncing

puritanical theology and allowing the divine warmth of love
free vent. In the same satiric vein he says that wine (102)
has rotted his high reputation as a theologian and astronomer,
also (62) that despite his wide learning he refuses to recognize
as valid any condition short of drunkenness—meaning any
loveless religious concept; also that he is growing too old now
(103) to start life from a new beginning and steadfastly refuses
to call himself a philosopher (63). Yet (109) he turns on those
who have taken the false road in regarding God as a cruel
and pitiless taskmaster, and who, having unknowingly
damned themselves by this blasphemous view, now offer
prayers for poor Khayaam's salvation—'nudging his mercy
from the Merciful'. Despite all his sins of omission or
commission (110) he never at least fell into the old Persian
heresy of worshipping a God whose nature combined Good
with Evil, one who was other than a God of Love and Mercy.
Khayaam does not attempt to define love, except as an
ecstatic influence that overcomes him and makes him both
the giver and the receiver.

Idries Shah relates that his great-great-grandfather Khan
Jan-Fishan-Khan, a nineteenth-century Grand Sheikh of the
Sufi *Tariqa*, used the *Rubaiyyat* in his Hindu Kush
principality for testing the capacities of new disciples. This
was made easier because his own version, he knew, contained
no extraneous material but was written by a single hand: as
he also knew the names and fames of smiths who had forged
the swords borne by his ancestors in the Crusades. So the
Rubaiyyat has been for more than eight hundred years an
integral part of the Sufis' poetic heritage and what is more,

Khayaam's secret use of special linguistic forms can be decoded for us only by Sufic initiates.

It is recorded that three new students once came to the Khan who, having received them kindly, told them to go away, read the *Rubaiyyat* with care and presently report on him. They came back on his next Day of Audience. The first disciple reported that he had been made to think as he had never thought before; the second, that Khayaam appeared to be a heretic; the third, that the poem contained a deep mystery which he hoped one day to understand. The first was kept as a disciple; the second was passed on to another Sheikh; the third was sent back to study Khayaam for another week.

An elder disciple then asked the Khan whether appreciation of the *Rubaiyyat* was a reliable touchstone for assessing the capacities of the uninitiated. The Khan replied: 'Intuition had already informed me somewhat about their capacities. But what I did was both a test and a part of their education, besides teaching those of you who watched the process. Sufism combines personal study and feeling with the interaction of active minds.'

It should be remembered that hard liquor was unknown to twelfth-century Persians and that Fitzgerald lived in a peculiarly sodden age. He therefore suggested that to use wine as a metaphor of love

'among so inflammable people as the Persians was hazardous both to the poet himself and to his weaker brethren; and even worse for the profane in proportion

as the devotion of the initiated grew warmer. And all for
what? To be tantalized with images of sensual enjoyment
which must be renounced if one would approximate a
God; yet without hope of a posthumous Beatitude in
another world to compensate for all one's self-denying
in this.'

However, at the end of his preface to the *Rubaiyyat*,
Fitzgerald does make a gentlemanly bow in the direction of
his rival, M. Nicolas, and admit that since certain learned men
favour the tradition of Omar's having been a Sufi, those who
please may so interpret his Wine and his Cupbearer. We bow
gravely in return, but do not, so to speak, wash Fitzgerald's
dead body in wine.

A main confusion in orthodox Moslem thought was
derived, Khayaam is suggesting, from an anthropomorphic
view of God as the Universal Father. He had been presented
first as stooping to mould man from clay in His own image
(82); then as knowing that sin is at once wrong and irresistible,
though ordering man to abstain from it (83) under pain of
Hell; finally as spreading snares (85) to catch him wherever
he goes, while still calling him a rebel if he gets caught.
Such a concept of God, Khayaam holds, necessarily draws
from enlightened man the scornful question (88); 'Say, am
I sinful? Are you not my Master? Did you not sin when you
created man?'

Fitzgerald deprecates this apparent infidelity, not recog-
nizing Khayaam's demand for a purer view of God as
perceptible under an infinity of disguises (57).

Hidden you live, inscrutable as ever—
A person sometimes, but sometimes a place,
Showing this costly spectacle to no one—
You, the sole audience and the actor too.

This view had been succinctly expressed in the anti-Gnostic
First Epistle of St. John IV, 7:

'He that loveth not, knoweth not God: for God is love.'

Which reminds me that, according to the Pharisee sage Hillel,
President of the Sanhedrin in Jesus's youth, the Mosaic
injunction: 'Love thy neighbour as thyself' was the most
important commandment in the Torah; for whoever did not
so love his neighbour would be unable to fulfil the
complementary commandment: 'Thou shalt love thy God
with all thy soul and strength.'

Khayaam's most biting sarcasm falls on the seventy-two
sects of Islam, all argumentatively chopping logic about the
Divine Nature: for seventy-two was the number of letters in
God's secret and ineffable Name—a mystery, as I have
suggested in my *White Goddess*, of Egyptian calendar origin,
passed on to the Moslems by the Jews.

Nevertheless, we should not be wholly ungrateful to
Fitzgerald for his mispresentation of Omar Khayaam; if
only because the widespread excitement generated by his
mumpsimus encourages a *sumpsimus*, a corrective presentation
of the true Khayaam—and this at a time when far more
readers will be prepared to welcome him than in Fitzgerald's
lifetime. Orthodox Christian disapproval of Moslem thought

is now no longer a serious barrier to such an acceptance; *fin-de-siècle* Victorian hedonism is equally out of fashion; and a poetic, rather than a theological, concept of God has been fast gaining ground throughout the Western world.

One point that should be made clear is that nowadays no reputable metaphysician, astronomer or mathematician can become a true poet as Khayaam did, or vice-versa. Such a feat would imply a total reversal of lifelong mental conditioning. That Khayaam could compose the *Rubaiyyat* in middle age, not in the graceful Horatian style of modern ex-Judges or Government Ministers, but as a whole-hearted and skilful poet, shows that Science had not yet ceased to be a Humanity. It did not, indeed, do so until at least the thirteenth century; but by the end of the seventeenth had become a self-perpetuating mechanical process which involved the disciplined brain, not the free heart and mind. Science is now increasingly dependent for support on Governmental or institutional finance, and therefore dedicated, in the main, to findings which can be industrially exploited; and thus deprive still more craftsmen of their former pride in manufacture—for 'manufacture' originally meant making things with one's own hands. The Sufic view of *baraka*, or blessedness, being passed on by potters, smiths, carpenters and other true craftsmen by their creations, and thus spiritually enlightening the houses where they are in use, throws light on what is technically termed the 'fatigue reactions' caused by modern commercial furnishing, art, music, literature, theatrical entertainment, food and entertainment, including many highly expendable popular love lyrics.

I end with a fugitive quatrain in which Khayaam refers to
the secret meaning of Sufic speech:

> Conceal the mystery revealed to you
> From all nonentities, likewise from fools:
> In carefulness approach men's inner selves,
> Letting none intercept your scrutiny.

HISTORICAL PREFACE
OMAR ALI-SHAH

'My Translation will interest you, very unliteral as
it is. Many Quatrains are mashed together and
something lost, I doubt, of Omar's Simplicity,
which is such a Virtue in him.'
(*Edward Fitzgerald to Professor Cowell, September 1858.*)

In preparing this translation and commentary with Robert
Graves's help, I have tried to present a 'standard' edition of
Sheikh Omar Khayaam's original *Rubaiyyat*, freed at last of
all accretions, interpolations and misunderstandings.

Though the *Rubaiyyat* was clearly written for readers with
a grounding in the Sufi lore to which it traditionally belongs,
a stubborn rear-guard of Oriental and Occidental scholars
will doubtless continue to cite alleged instances of Khayaam's
anti-Sufic verses. This will be simply because the poem's
technical terms, semantic nuances and argumentative *judo*—
obvious enough to readers trained in the Sufic way of thinking
—baffle and provoke natural resentment in non-initiates.

Edward Fitzgerald once wrote to his friend and mentor
Professor Cowell: 'Persian is certainly a very beautiful
language so far as words go, but its grammar is sadly
defective.' That was in July 1857, after Fitzgerald had busied
himself for some four years in studying this very complex
language, with the poor help of Johnson's Persian–English
dictionary—from which, we are told, he always picked the

meaning nearest to his intuitive guess of what a passage demanded.

Here are three of Fitzgerald's intuitions, picked at random from scores that occur in his correspondence with Cowell:

> June 1857: '*Nuh* must be the mystical shout of the Dervish.' (*The word is, in fact, na'ara or 'cry'.*)
> June 1857: 'I think it is said the Sufis bore Omar a great grudge.' (*This is hearsay, and quite untrue.*)
> August 1857: '*U Danad* may be some technical call in Polo.' (*U Danad, stanza 50 in Fitzgerald's Second Edition, 74 in our manuscript, is the third person singular present indicative of the verb* danistan—*to know—and means, simply: 'he knows'.*)

Yet Fitzgerald considered himself sufficient of a Persian expert to dismiss the poet Jelaluddin Rumi, fourteenth-century author of the *Mathnavi*, with a typical insularism:

> 'I don't speak of Jelal, whom I know so little of, but enough to show me he is no great Artist.'

In a way Fitzgerald was right. Rumi was not a 'great artist' in the mid-Victorian sense of literary artistry, but ranks with the few true poets of West and East. As for Khayaam, the game of 'attribution' that scholars have played with his authentic or alleged verses, since Fitzgerald awoke their interest in them, does not greatly interest me. The present translation is made from a twelfth-century manuscript of uncontradictable authority, whose existence has been known for centuries. I cannot claim that its one hundred and eleven verses form the complete corpus of Khayaam's *Rubaiyyat*, only that these are poetically the most important ones; that they all occur in one or more of the earlier MSS housed in libraries throughout the world; and that none of them is blasphemous, atheistic or anti-Sufi in content. Finally, that Khayaam's Sufi connections form part of the oral tradition which has been handed down in my family for the last nine centuries.

Sheikh Ghiathuddin Abdul Fath Omar ibn Ibrahim al Khayaam al Ghaq was born at Nishapur in A.D. 1015, of Afghan parents from the Sufi community at Balkh where, according to Shahrazuri, Papazai and others, the family originated. His own teacher, Sheikh Mawaffikuddin, certainly belonged to the Qadiri order; but the popular story of how this 'poor but honest' lad was charitably taken on by Sheikh Mawaffikuddin, whose other pupils were the sons of nobles, can be disproved: Khayaam's family, it is known, was neither plebeian nor impoverished. His poetic *takhallus* or pen-name, 'Tentmaker', is a Sufic one and if decoded by the *abjad* system reveals the Sufic name 'Al Ghaqi' or 'Squanderer of goods' (see note on p. 77). Most Sufi sheikhs and teachers took similarly encoded pen-names, many of these referring to the actual craft to which, on the advice of their Sheikhs, they had dedicated their lives.

The Western view of Khayaam—'a man of rudest wit and shallowest reputation . . . lean and flashy songs . . . tipsy toper, purblind beggar' (Dr. Hastie)—'blasphemer, a poet of rationalist pessimism' (Professor Arberry)—'author of irreligious and antinomian utterances' (E. H. Whinfield)—

contrasts oddly with that of Khayaam's Eastern contemporaries who were, after all, in a better position to judge him than his modern detractors. The devout prosodist Nizami, for instance, styléd him 'Argument of Truth' and 'Imam' (religious leader or scholar).

I agree with Robert Graves that Fitzgerald's famous mistranslation happened to fill a late nineteenth-century need for anti-devotional or defeatist verse; and it often happens that an unsuccessful writer pirates another's work and debases it to capture a contemporary market. Fitzgerald is, however, no longer alive to plead his case and, even if he were, our historical judgement would still be Qasim Yaghistani's:

> 'He was a poet neither in soul, fame nor conscience. Must not his reputation now suffer proportionately to the harm he has done Khayaam—a poet, mathematician and philosopher whose gigantic powers accentuate his translator's own littleness?'

Nor would Fitzgerald, in his earlier years at least, have had much to offer in self-defence beyond what appears in a letter written on February 21st, 1842:

> 'I have not the strong inward call, nor cruel sweet pangs of parturition that prove the birth of anything bigger than a mouse.'

Edward Fitzgerald is not the only Westerner for whom the meaning of the *Rubaiyyat* has seemed too obscure for accurate translation into English; yet E. H. Whinfield, as a Khayaam

expert, dismisses the possibility that it contains any secret
Sufic doctrine. He states, though unhistorically, that 'this
symbolism was not formulated in Omar's time'. On a
previous page, however, he has conceded that 'most of the
verses probably bear a mystic meaning'. He refrains from
suggesting what sort of mysticism this was, but leaves himself
room for tactical retreat; and has at least been generous
enough to admit that 'whatever Omar Khayaam was, he was
no atheist'.

Fitzgerald's charge of atheism was repeated as recently as
1952 by Professor Arberry (*Omar Khayaam, a New Version
Based upon Recent Discoveries*). In citing Fitzgerald's opening verse
(*Awake, for morning* etc.) he held that the last line, which the
memory of a mystical legend had induced Khayaam to write,
displayed 'his characteristic touch of blasphemy'. According
to this legend the Saki ('cup-bearer') of God the Lover
poured wine for God the Beloved on forty successive mornings.
Arberry makes out that Khayaam's use of the priestly Arabic
word for 'drink', *ishrabu*, instead of the ordinary Persian verb,
bukhor, indicated the divine nature of the command and
recalled the Koranic *surah* 'Eat and drink the good things . . .'
He argues therefore that this introduction of God into a
wine-shop scene supplies a clear example of Khayaam's
'outrageous wit'. Yet the legend is not, as it happens, implied
in this verse, where no pious Persian has ever detected the
least touch of blasphemy.

Professor Arberry also finds blasphemy in Khayaam's use
(our verse 27) of *Burak*—the winged steed, mounted on
which the Prophet Mohammed made his celebrated Night

Journey to heaven. Yet in orthodox Islamic theology the steed, whether regarded as real or metaphorical, is only 'respected', not worshipped as a divine being. Thus the use of its name to express a flight of ecstatic thought cannot be considered blasphemous. Arberry is perhaps trying to avoid being charged with blasphemy in his own translation: for he substitutes 'Speculation's steed' for *Burak*—thus unfortunately reducing the Prophet's experience from mystic reality to scientific speculation. Another puzzling choice of equine terminology appears in Arberry's verse 34 (our 17) where he translates *ablak* ('piebald steed') as 'poor hack'.

Fitzgerald seems to have been the first writer either in the West or East to present Khayaam as a blasphemer. He did so, I think, partly because he knew so little Persian; partly also because he realized that daring drawing-room verse, if both foreign enough and ancient enough, would cause the strait-laced mid-Victorian reading public delightful *frissons* of trepidation; but mainly because he did not realize that Khayaam, in his Sufic scorn for Orthodox believers, whose anthropomorphic view of God led to real blasphemy, was satirically impersonating them. His verse 30 in his Second Edition (based on our 32) runs:

> What, without asking, hither hurried whence?
> And, without asking, whither hurried hence!
> Another and another cup to drown
> The Memory of this impertinence.

Yet the original manuscript contains no mention of such compulsive hurrying, still less of any impertinence. Even the widest poetic licence can hardly empower a translator so to deface the sense of a poem as to dishonour its author's integrity.

One of Fitzgerald's most celebrated verses (58) makes Khayaam adjure God to seek man's forgiveness:

> O Thou who Man of baser Earth didst make,
> And who with Eden didst devise the Snake;
> For all the Sin wherewith the Face of Man
> Is blacken'd, Man's Forgiveness give—and take!

Yet Khayaam's original verse (our 87) mentions neither Earth nor Eden, Snake nor Sin, and asks God for forgiveness without volunteering a similar courtesy.

Fitzgerald's verse 94 (our 89):

> Whereat some one of the loquacious Lot—
> I think a Sufi pipkin waxing hot—
> 'All this of Pot and Potter—Tell me then
> Who is the Potter, pray, and who the Pot?'

does not match the original, which contains neither Sufi nor pipkin nor any question of identity.

His verse 64 makes Khayaam once more trespass on the field of blasphemy with:

> Said one—'Folks of a surly Tapster tell,
> And daub his visage with the Smoke of Hell;
> They talk of some strict testing of us—Pish!
> He's a Good Fellow, and 'twill all be well'.

On consulting the original verse (our 94) readers will be tempted to echo the 'pish' and ask:

> Where is the Tapster, pray, and where the Hell
> Findst thou Hell's Smoke? We know this Stanza well!

It is not easy for me, who as a child read and spoke classical Persian, to have patience with Western mistranslations of Khayaam. I feel outraged by such wilful ignorance combined with the crooked manipulation of verses to make them fit alien patterns of thought. Yet I must assume a phlegmatic air, even when E. H. Whinfield, as guardian of the people's morals, takes it upon himself to 'exclude from this translation a number of quatrains in praise of wine, and exhortations to live for the day, which occur in the manuscript with the most wearisome frequency'. Or when Professor Arberry, now Professor of Arabic at Cambridge University, writes of Fitzgerald in *A New Version of the Rubaiyyat Based upon Recent Discoveries*, 'it would be a great impertinence, and would betray a singular perversity of taste, to make the attempt to belittle the greatness of a Victorian genius'. Surely the impertinence and perversity of taste were Fitzgerald's own, in belittling a pre-Victorian genius? And if I err in tarnishing Fitzgerald's halo, I must plead that the truthful rendering of an ancient poem, especially when the poet happens to have been my compatriot, is more important to me than the posthumous reputation of a dilettante who owed his literary fame to deliberate misrepresentations not only of Khayaam and Jami (*Salaman and Absal*) but also of Aeschylus and Calderón.

According to Thomas Wright (*Life of Edward Fitzgerald*, 1904) Professor Cowell, who introduced Fitzgerald to Khayaam, held that Khayaam was a Sufi and that his writings were mystical; whereas Fitzgerald himself 'sometimes thought Omar to have been a Sufi, and sometimes not. He could never make up his mind.' Apparently the appearance of J. B. Nicolas's French translation of the *Rubaiyyat* which, as Robert Graves mentions, appeared between the publication of Fitzgerald's first and second editions, pushed him into a decision. Nicolas had learned that Khayaam was a Sufi, and Fitzgerald reacted by an outright denial that this was so. For that matter, he had also expressed himself 'unconvinced of the Mysticism of Hafiz'; which made him the only so-called expert to adopt the view. Yet M. Nicolas, as French Consul at Resht, was in touch with far better informed opinion than Fitzgerald—especially now that Professor Cowell was away in India and had left him with no more serviceable guide to the intricacies of Sufic poetry than Johnson's Persian-English dictionary.

Robert Graves has posed a question regarding the sources used by Fitzgerald. He points out that the arrangement of the verses in the First Edition vary greatly from that in the subsequent ones. Here one can only say that Fitzgerald is reputed to have used both the Bodleian (Ouseley) manuscript and a Bengal Asiatic Society, Calcutta manuscript, the original of which is lost, and that the copy which Professor Cowell had made for Fitzgerald is the only extant version. We know nothing of the antecedents of this manuscript and it is quite possible that it was a compendium of verses from various manuscripts in India and that Fitzgerald, or Cowell, had access to yet another manuscript, or copy of one, which more closely followed the arrangement of the A.D. 1153 manuscript which I have used. Another book could be written about the various manuscripts, their authenticity or lack of it, and the arrangement of the verses, but such a study is outside the scope of this volume, although in the process of being made.

I find it hard to believe that, in support of Fitzgerald's sacred intuitions, serious scholars can honestly offer the far-fetched theory that later Sufis disingenuously adopted this blasphemer Khayaam and presented him to the world as one of themselves! Moreover, the accident that a single biased writer, Qifti, who wrote a *History of the Philosophers* a century after Khayaam's death, accused him of unSufic thought, does not outbalance the immense weight of contrary evidence. In Khayaam's day, and afterwards, non-initiates and enemies of Sufism abounded, and his prestige must have tempted occasional thirteenth-century dissidents to malign him. But that Qifti's off-beat view has convinced so many Western scholars is perhaps not surprising: Christians resent the claim of Islam that Jesus was a mere prophetic predecessor of Mohammed, far more than the Jews' downright denial of his Messiahship: and are the readier to believe that one of Islam's most famous poets was an unbeliever. We are reminded of Henry Festing Jones's outraged remark to Samuel Butler: 'Not even God can change history!' and Butler's dry answer: 'No, Jones: only historians can do that.'

Professor Arberry remarks that 'none but the less dis-criminating admirers of the poet hold the theory put out by

M. Nicolas', namely, that Khayaam must be interpreted allegorically—but M. Nicolas was not the first, by several centuries, to put out this theory in the East or West. Among the 'less discriminating', Arberry has unwittingly included several million Sufis, and all native-born experts in Persian language and literature. He also charges Sultan Mahmud of Ghazna, whom he names that 'awe-inspiring Turkish bigot' (*New Version Based upon Recent Discoveries*, p. 29), with regarding Islamic orthodoxy as the only safe way of life. This charge is offered in support of a novel theory that Khayaam's *Rubaiyyat* was secretly quoted by members of the 'Persian revolt against religious conformity'. Yet it is undeniable that Sultan Mahmud attracted to his court a great array of poets, scholars and savants who 'shed a glorious lustre on his brilliant reign' (Professor Ameer Ali, P.C., *The Spirit of Islam*— *Encyc. Brit.*) and that Mahmud was the patron of Al Beiruni, Firdousi and Dakiki—strange courtiers for a religious bigot! And the celebrated Sufic Imam Al Ghazali is accused by Arberry (*op. cit.*, p. 30) of 'putting an end to free speculation of Islam'—the truth being that the sheer excellence of Ghazali's dialectic and logic silenced all his contemporaries, that his mind worked from free thought to certitude, and that the coherence of his views has never since been faulted.

These instances of Professor Arberry's novel opinions are made to support a view that Khayaam's poetry was 'whispered about' and that its 'libertine' and 'Persian' character made it an effective reply to the 'foreign and not very clever Arabian creed' which, he tells us, was how the Persians viewed Islam! Yet, Khayaam's verses were neither libertine nor Epicurean, and possessed no quality which disparaged Islam. And it is with a covert sneer that Arberry quotes Baihaqi the historian:

> 'Baihaqi has Khayaam die in an odour of sanctity, quoting as his last words the prayer: "O God, Thou art aware that I have known Thee to the full extent of my powers. Forgive me, for my knowledge of Thee is my means of coming to Thee!" '

But since Shahrazuri in his thirteenth-century *Nuhsatal Arwah* quotes these same last words, why should Professor Arberry suggest that Baihaqi is guilty of a pious fraud? Has the desire to prove Khayaam a blasphemous agnostic once more disturbed his historical judgement?

A recent unsigned contribution to the new American-owned *Encyclopaedia Britannica* declares that much of Khayaam's poetry was 'directed against the wild ravings of the Sufis'; which shows how subjective opinion can cloud popular knowledge by spilling over into what was once a dependable reference book. It is as though the Baconian theory of the authorship of Shakespeare's plays had been similarly approved by the editors. Yet Oriental scholars cannot be wholly acquitted of mistelling the Khayaam story: for example, Qifti and Shirazi have both tried to establish an untenable view of Sheikh Omar's descent from the Arab tribe of Khayaam.

Here let me quote from the standard work of Sufism, *The Sufis,* by Idries Shah.

> 'While it has been generally accepted that Khayaam was a poet without much honour in his own country

until reintroduced by the esteem which Fitzgerald's translation caused in the West, this again is not strictly accurate. Khayaam, it is true, was not so universally prized as Saadi, Hafiz, Rumi and other Sufi poets; the function of the collection of poems which passes under his name was slightly different. It is doubtful whether any Sufis were asked by Westerners what they thought of Khayaam. And it must be admitted that, even if they were asked, few of them would have cared to discuss the matter with an outsider . . .

'Khayaam is the Sufi voice; and the Sufi voice, to the Sufi, is timeless. In poetry it will not submit readily to time-centred theories. That Khayaam has been re-discovered in Persia through the fame of Fitzgerald's translation is true—if we amend this to read "Khayaam was not well known to non-Sufis in Persia until compara-tively recently. However, through the efforts of Western scholars, his work has become very widely known to them.'"

Indeed, the Moslem divine Molvi Khanzada, dismayed by the extent to which Fitzgerald's translation had misled English-speaking Indian Moslems, felt obliged to warn them that it should be read with considerable reservations. To begin with, he said, Fitzgerald did not know much Persian and neither did his teacher, Professor Cowell ('both scrawled badly like small children'). Next, those who wished to read Khayaam ought first to study Persian at length and only then, with a full knowledge of Islam, approach such weighty matters as Sufic thought. Finally, 'Khayaam' should be treated as a generic term for a Sufic way of teaching which is necessarily misleading unless learned with the guidance of an accepted sheikh.

Idries Shah also discusses the 'Saki' who appears so often in the *Rubaiyyat*. He explains that, in Sufi literature, the Saki may appear as an actual person where one is needed to fulfil a cupbearer's function, but often is no more than an impersonal abstraction on which to hang the verse.

I can add little of biographical interest to what is already known of Sheikh Omar Khayaam. All the world has read of Khayaam's life-long friendship with his benefactor Nizam ul Mulk, Wazir of Alp Arslan, and with Hassan ibn Sabbah, the Assassin Sheikh: how Omar repaid Nizam's generosity with remarkable mathematical research and a new Moslem calendar, but Hassan with a poisoned dagger.

Khayaam's fame has survived various unfounded charges of crime and perversity. I hold to our family tradition that his love was centred on Halima Begum, daughter of an official at Alp Arslan's court, whose hand was denied to him because she had been betrothed to another man in infancy. Omar brought no pressure to bear on her parents, as a lesser man might have done in his privileged circumstances, but honoured the bond and asked no more than the love that he drew from spiritual union with Halima. He is said never to have betrayed this love by any unguarded word or deed; yet his poems bear the unmistakable stamp of one whose Muse was for ever sacred to him. He lived, wrote and died still true to the traditional virtues of his noble house. Some

may dispute the authenticity of his last prayer, but none can
dispute that of his self-epitaph:

> Though pearls in praise of God I never strung,
> Though dust of sin lies clotted on my brow,
> Yet will I not despair of mercy. When
> Did Omar argue that the One was Two?

THE RUBAIYYAT

NOTE. *The numbers in the first column are those of the verses as they appear, in sequence, in the authentic MS. The numbers in the second column are the equivalent verses, where they occur, in Fitzgerald's First Edition; while the third column refers to his second and subsequent revisions.*

1 While Dawn, Day's herald straddling the whole sky,   1   1
   Offers the drowsy world a toast 'To Wine',
   The Sun spills early gold on city roofs—
   Day's regal Host, replenishing his jug.

2 Then shouts ring out among us at the tavern: 2
   'Rise too, you good-for-nothing tavern lad!
   Refill our empty bowls with today's measure
   Before the measure of our lives be filled!'

3 'Loud crows the cock for his dawn drink, my Saki!'   3   3
   'Here stand we in the Vinter's Row, my Saki!'
   'Is this an hour for prayer? Silence, my Saki!'
   'Defy old custom, Saki; drink your fill!'

4 Rarest of lads, rising to greet the dawn;   3   3
   Favour my bowl of crystal, pour red wine!
   This moment filched from the grey corpse of night
   We long may sigh for, never repossess.

5 Now that our world finds riches within reach,   4   4
    Live hearts awake and hanker for wide plains
    Where every bough is blanched by Moses-hand
    And every breeze perfumed by Jesus-breath.

6 A glorious morning, neither hot nor dank,   6   6
    With cheeks of roses newly bathed in dew;
    The nightingale, in Pahlevi, prescribes
    For every sallower cheek: 'Wine, wine and wine!'

7 Most guiltily each morning I determine   102   70
    From wine in bowl or goblet to abstain;
    But this is rose-time—Lord, why should I blush
    So soon of my repentance to repent?

8 Life passes. What is Balkh? what is Baghdad?   8   39
    The cup fills—should we care whether with bitter
    Or sweet? Drink on! Know that long after us
    The Moon must keep her long-determined course.

9 Rest in the rose's shade, though winds have burst   9   8
   A world of blossom; petals fall to dust—
   Jamsheds and Khusros by the hundred thousand
   Lie tumbled by a similar stroke of time.

10 One ample draught outdoes the fame of Kawus,   10   9
   Kobad the Glorious or Imperial Tus.
   Friend, never bow your neck even to Rustum
   Nor proffer thanks even to Hatim Tai.

11 Should our day's portion be one mancel loaf,   11   11
   A haunch of mutton and a gourd of wine
   Set for us two alone on the wide plain,
   No Sultan's bounty could evoke such joy.

12 A gourd of red wine and a sheaf of poems—   12   11
   A bare subsistence, half a loaf, not more—
   Supplied us two alone in the free desert:
   What Sultan could we envy on his throne?

13   They say that Eden is bejewelled with houris;   13   12
     I answer that grape-nectar has no price—
     So laugh at long-term credit, stick to coin,
     Though distant drums beguile your greedy ear.

14   The Rose cried: 'I am generous of largesse   15   13
     And laughter. Laughingly my petals blow
     Across the world; the ribbons of my purse
     Snap and its load of coin flies everywhere.'

15   Before Fate springs her ambush for your life,   15   15
     Command our tavern-lad to fetch you drink.
     Fool, your dry corpse will be no treasure trove
     For proud posterity to disinter!

16   Think of this world as modelled at your whim,   17   14
     Perfectly trimmed for you from east to west;
     Yet know yourself a snowdrift on the sand
     Heaped for two days or three, then thawed and gone.

17   This ruined caravanserai, called Earth—   18   16
      Stable of Day-with-Night, a piebald steed;
      Former pavilion of a hundred Jamsheds;
      A hundred Bahrams' one-time hall of state;

18   A Palace gorged in by gigantic Bahram—   19   17
      The vixen whelps there and the lion nods.
      Bahram, who hunted none but onagers,
      Lies tumbled in a pitfall called the grave.

19   Each rose or tulip bed that you encounter   24   18
      Is sure to mark a king's last resting-place,
      While scented violets, rising from black soil,
      Record the burial of some lovely girl.

20   Green cresses, also, masking a stream's bank   25   19
      Start up from creatures of angelic kind.
      Tread softly on such evidence of beauty:
      Red lips and rosy cheeks fast slumbering.

21 Never anticipate tomorrow's sorrow;   24   20
    Live always in this paradisal Now—
    Fated however soon to house, instead,
    With others gone these seven thousand years:

22 My tavern comrades vanish one by one,   22   21
    Innocent victims of Death's furtive stroke.
    All had been honest drinkers, but all failed,
    Two rounds before the last, to drain their bowls.

23 Rise up, why mourn this transient world of men?   22
    Pass your whole life in gratitude and joy.
    Had humankind been freed from womb and tomb,
    When would your turn have come to live and love?

24 Allow no shadow of regret to cloud you,   23
    No absurd grief to overcast your days.
    Never renounce love-songs, or lawns, or kisses
    Until your clay lies mixed with elder clay.

25 Some ponder long on doctrine and belief,   27   24
    Some teeter between certitude and doubt.
    Suddenly out of hiding leaps the Guide
    With: 'Fools, the Way is neither that nor this.'

26 Most of them, gone before we go, my Saki,   29   25
    Drowse in their dusty bed of pride, my Saki.
    Drink yet again and hear the truth at last:
    'Whatever words they spoke were wind, my Saki.'

27 Yet those who proved most perfect of our kind
    Mounted the soaring Burak of their thoughts.
    Study your essence: like the Firmament,
    Your head will turn and turn, vertiginously.

28 In childhood once we crouched before our teacher,   30   27
    Growing content, in time, with what he taught;
    How does the story end? What happened to us?
    We came like water and like wind were gone.

29   When falcon-like I darted from my world
     Of mystery, upward and upward flying,
     No sage stood there to greet me with the truth;
     So back I dived by the same narrow door.

30   Man's brain has never solved the eternal Why   26
     Nor foraged past the frontier set for thought.
     All intellect be sure, proves nugatory,
     However hard we either teach or learn.

31   In agitation I was brought to birth   32   29
     And learned nothing from life but wonder at it;
     Reluctantly we leave, still uninformed
     Why in the world we came, or went, or were.

32   My presence here has been no choice of mine;   30
     Fate hounds me most unwillingly away.
     Rise, wrap a cloth about your loins, my Saki,
     And swill away the misery of this world.

33   Were the choice mine to come, should I have come?
     Or to become? What might I have become?
     What better fortune could I then have chanced on
     Than not to come, become, or even be?

34   Earth's Perigee to Saturn's Apogee—   34   31
     I have unveiled all astral mysteries:
     Breaking the barriers of deceit and fraud,
     Leaping all obstacles but Fate's design.

35   Not you, not I, can learn the inmost secret: 35   32
     The eternal Cypher proves too hard to break.
     Behind God's Curtain voices babble of us
     But when it parts, where then shall we two be?

36   Greedily to the bowl my lips I pressed   38
     And asked how might I sue for green old age.
     Pressing its lips to mine it muttered darkly:
     'Drink up! Once gone, you shall return no more!'

37 This jug was, ages past, a doleful lover   39   35
    Like me—who had pursued a dream, like me.
    This handle at its neck was once an arm
    Entwined about some neck he loved too well.

38 Yesterday in the market stood a potter   40   36
    Pounding relentlessly his batch of clay.
    My inner ear could hear it sigh and groan:
    'Brother, I once was like you. Treat me gently!'

39 In the potter's workroom, shadowed by the wheel,
    I pondered, watching how the Master made
    Handles and covers for his jugs and pitchers
    From clay—from hands of kings, from beggars' feet.

40 I wandered further down the Potters' Row.   41
    Continuously they tried new skills on clay;
    Yet some, devoid of vision, never noted
    The ancestral dust on every turning wheel.

41 Each drop of wine that Saki negligently   42   44
    Spills on the ground may quench the fires of grief
    In some sore heart. All praise to Him who offers
    Such medicine to relieve its melancholy!

42 Raise the bowl high, like tulip-cups at Nauroz,   43
    And if the moon-faced one has time to spare
    Drink gloriously deep, for brutal Time
    Will strike you down with never a warning yell.

43 Avoid all greed and envy, unperturbed   44
    By permutations, foul succeeding fair;
    Possess your bowl, play with your loved one's curls;
    Soon the whole scene must vanish past recourse.

44 Khayaam, should you be drunk with love, rejoice!   45   47
    Or bedded with your heart's delight, rejoice!
    Your end is no more than the whole world's end.
    Fancy yourself no longer there; then smile.

45 Oppose all resurrections of your past,
    Resent no anguish still prepared for you,
    Dwell lightly on your entrance and your exit—
    Drink, never cast your essence to the winds.

46 This vast, unmeasured, universal vault   46   52
    Offers one bowl for all mankind to drink.   48
    When your turn comes, refrain from tears, be merry,
    Lift high the bowl, then drain it to its lees!

47 Dear love, when you are free to slough your skin   69
    And become naked spirit, soaring far
    Across God's Empyrean, you will blush
    That you lay cramped so long in body's gaol.

48 Khayaam, your mortal carcase is a tent;   70
    Your soul, a Sultan; and your camp, all Time.
    The groom called Fate maps out tomorrow's march
    And strikes the tent when, Sultan-like, you move.

49 Khayaam, though this blue-stained royal pavilion,   47
    Tautens its golden guy-ropes against entry,
    A deathless Saki draws Khayaams in thousands
    Like wine-bubbles out of Creation's bowl.

50 This world must long survive our poor departure,   48
    Persisting without name or note of us.
    Before we came, it never grudged our absence;
    When we have gone, how can it feel regret?

51 The caravan of life passes in strangeness.   49   38
    Come, seize one moment passing joyfully.
    Why mourn for friends and their tomorrow, Saki?
    Pour out more wine: the night is passing too.

52 Dear lad, steeped as you are in Mysteries,   55
    Why should you load your heart with nameless cares?
    Let projects fade away; disport yourself
    In the brief hour when life detains you here.

53 One breath parts infidelity from faith;   50
   Another breath parts certitude from doubt.
   Yet cherish breath, never make light of it—
   Is not such breath the harvest of our being?

54 My heart complained: 'I long for inspiration,   50
   I long for wisdom, to be taught and learn.'
   I breathed the letter A. My heart replied:
   'A is enough to occupy this house.'

55 The Moon, by her own nature skilled in change,   51
   Varies from animal form to vegetable.
   Destroy the form, you destroy nothingness—
   For what she seems survives her not-yet-being.

56 Bring wine to allay the fever of my heart;   52
   Existence here runs as quicksilver runs.
   Rise up, for wakefulness is what sleep treasures
   And fires of youth like water drain away.

57 Hidden you live, inscrutable as ever—
    A person sometimes, but sometimes a place,
    Showing this costly spectacle to no one—
    You, the sole audience and the actor too.

58 Could my heart know, in life, life's hidden secrets,   54   37
    Death could inform me of God's hidden secrets.
    Since I know nothing of myself today,
    What can I know tomorrow, after death?

59 Those dupes of intellect and logic die   56
    In arguments on being or not being;
    Go, ignoramus, choose your vintage well—
    From dust like theirs grow none but unripe grapes.

60 Eternity eternally discussed!   55
    In hours of joy wine will not play us false.
    Knowledge and practice lie beyond our scope
    But wine solves all enigmas that obtrude.

61   I shall possess myself of a great goblet   57   40
        With pipes of wine for its replenishment,
        Annulling former ties to Faith and Reason
        By marriage with this daughter of the Vine.

62   As one familiar with all exoterics   58   41
        Of being and not-being, who has plumbed
        The abyss of shame, how can I greet as valid
        Any condition short of drunkenness?

63   Misguided foes call me philosopher—
        God knows this is the one thing I am not.
        I am even less: in such a nest of sorrows
        I cannot tell you even who I am.

64   In drink this evening, as I passed the tavern,   42
        A fellow toper met me with a flask.
        Cried I: 'Old man, have you no awe of God?'
        'Come', he said, 'God is bountiful! Come, drink!'

65   Banish your crowding griefs with wine, disperse   61   43
      Your memories of the two-and-seventy sects
      And praise wine's alchemy that still can banish
      With one red draught more than a thousand spites.

66   I drink wine as my fellow-topers drink.
      How much I drink can seem of small concern
      To God, who knows well that I drink. Abstention
      From drink would make God's knowledge ignorance.

67   They say: 'Be sober, lest you die of drink   56
      And earn Hell fire on God's Last Judgement Day.'
      Nevertheless my blaze of drunkenness
      Outshines both worlds: your Now and your Hereafter.

68   My wandering feet have led me through far plains   67
      And valleys: I have strayed this way and that
      Yet never found a traveller who could boast
      That he had ever trod the same road twice.

69   Exemplars of the cultured and genteel   68
      Though moulding candles from these predicates
      Have never lighted one to mark the way
      By night; but told their fables and slept on.

70   Already at Creation I stretched out   71
      For Pen and Tablet, also Heaven and Hell;
      But prudently my Teacher warned me: 'Pen
      And Tablet, Heaven and Hell, lie in yourself.'

71   My broken body serves the Sky for girdle,   72
      My precious tears carved out the Jihun's bed;
      Hell is the furnace for my suffering soul;
      Paradise, my one moment of release.

72   This vault, underneath which we live bemused   73   52
      Is, so to speak, God's magic shadow-show: 76
      With sun for lamp, the world as a wide screen
      For countless lie-rehearsing silhouettes.

66

73   Let me speak out, unallegorically: 74   49
     We are mere puppets of our Master, toys
     On the Table of Existence, one by one
     Flung back in the toy box of Non-existence.

74   Poor ball, struck by Fate's heavy polo-mallet,   75   50
     Running whichever way it drives you, numbed
     Of sense, though He who set you on your course,
     He knows, He knows, He knows.

75   What we shall be is written, and we are so.   76   51
     Heedless of God or Evil, pen, write on!   53
     By the first day all futures were decided;
     Which gives our griefs and pains irrelevancy.

76   Evil and Good dispute the heart's possession;   78   52
     Sorrow and Joy are man's predestined lot.
     Live in no awe of planets. Planets are
     One thousand times more impotent than we.

77   Truth is hyperbole, my heart of hearts.
     Why are you so distressed by grief and labour?
     Yield to your destiny, conform, conform!
     Tomorrow too is framed by destiny.

78   Yesterday they determined your today   80
     Exempt from yesterday's inept desires.
     Rejoice that by no effort of your own
     Tomorrow also is mapped out for you.

79   But while the Eternal One created me   82   55
     He word by word spelt out my lesson, love,
     And seized my heart and from a fragment cut
     Keys to the storehouse of Reality.

80   When first the Sky's wild horses won their saddles,   81   54
     When Jupiter first blazed, the Pleiads too,
     My fate was published from God's Judgement seat.
     How can I err? I act as it is written.

81　Mysteries broached with joy in tavern talk　　　　　83
　　Have far more substance than a mumbled prayer
　　To you, my Last and First, my soul's Creator
　　Empowered either to sear or succour me.

82　When, bending low, God moulded me from clay,　　84
　　Incontrovertibly my life was ordered:
　　Without His order I abstain from crime.
　　Why should I burn, then, on His Judgement Day?

83　That sin is irresistible, He knows;　　　　　　　85
　　Yet He commands us to abstain from sin.
　　Thus irresistibility confounds us
　　With prohibition:—'Lean, but never fall!'

84　The clay from which this human frame was moulded
　　Forewarned a hundred wonders for me; yet—
　　Could I be worse or better than I am
　　Who was, even before He fashioned me?

85 On every path I take, Your snares are spread
     To entrap me, should I walk without due care.
     Utter extremes acknowledge Your vast sway.
     You order all things—yet You call me rebel?

86 If sinfully I drudge, where is Your mercy?
     If clouds darken my heart, where is Your light?
     Heaven rewards my practice of obedience;
     Rewards well-earned are good—but what of grace?

87 You, always cognisant of every secret;
     Who succour all flesh in its hour of need,
     Grant me repentance, grant me mercy too—
     You who forgive all, You who punish all,

88 Ordaining every cause for life or death,
     Guarding this tattered robe we call the Sky,
     Say, am I sinful? Are you not my Master?
     Who sins when You alone created me?

89   I saw at least two thousand pots, last night   94   59
      In Potters Row, not all of which were mute,   60
      And one cried loudly: 'Friends, where is the Potter,
      Where is the salesman, where the customer?'

90   Ramazan's moon, I hear, rides high again.   89   59
      Soon none may give new rein to hot desire;
      Yet before Shaban ends, I shall have drunk
      Sweet wine enough to float me through that Fast.

91   There is one bowl praised by the wide wise world   92   61
      That tempts a toper to a hundred kisses;
      And yet the Potter moulds this fragile clay
      Only to fall and shatter on the ground.

92   The elements that constitute a bowl   62
      Hate all besotted murderers of bowls—
      Bowls deftly moulded for the love of whom?
      Then dashed to pieces, as a curse on whom?

71

93   Our Guardian chose our natures. Is He then   93   63
     Delinquent when He treats us with disorder?
     We ask: 'Why break the best of us?' and murmur:
     'Is the pot guilty if it stands awry?'

94   Though Judgement Day should prove a grand ordeal   95   64
     Handled, they say, by a short-tempered Judge,
     Yet never fear: good has the final word—
     Nothing of Evil can proceed from Good.

95   When this existence finds an end at last,   96   65
     When all I am scatters to the four winds,
     Let them remould me as a jug, that then
     I may revive, well soused in glorious drink.

96   When Destiny, I say, has trod me down
     Cutting my root of hope, sweet friends, assemble
     And from my clay contrive a single jug
     To thrive again, well soused in glorious drink.

97   Shawal is with us, Ramazan has passed.   *97*
      Salute the month of joy and lutes and singing.
      When wineskins for the shoulder cry aloud:
      'Here come the porters, one after another!'

98   Should I fall dead, wash my poor corpse in wine;   *98*   *65*
      Read it into the grave with drinking songs.
      On Judgement Day, if you have need of me,
      Delve in the soil beneath our tavern door.

99   Take heed to pamper me with bowls that change
      A pasty-coloured cheek to ruby red.   *67*
      When I fall dead, I say, wash me in wine
      And use the vine's own slats for coffin-wood.

100 So lovingly I drink, the wine's bouquet   *100*   *68*
      Will scent the air where I lie underground;
      A toper treading past my grave will pause
      To sniff, and find himself ignobly drunk.

101   Once, years ago, inclined to prayer and fasting   69
      I swore my soul was free and given to God.
      Alas for purity once more besmirched—
      For a vow broken by one sip of wine!

102   Though drink has rotted my high reputation,   103   71
      Reject it I will not, while I yet breathe,
      Wondering often what the vinters buy
      Equal in value with the wine they sell.

103   Ah me, the book of early glory closes,   104   72
      The green of Spring makes way for wintry snow.
      The cheerful bird of Youth flutters away—
      I hardly noticed how it came or went.

104   If only I could find some tranquil spot   105
      For sleep; if only this long road would end!
      If only from some inner core of earth
      We might spring up once more to bud and blossom!

105   If only I controlled God's Universe,   108   73
      Would I not wipe away these faulty Heavens
      And build from nothing a true Paradise
      Where all souls could achieve their hearts' desire?

106   Since no voice here can promise you tomorrow,   109   74
      Content yourself, my mortal Moon, with bowls
      Emptied by moonlight—one fine night the Moon
      May search the world for us, but find us gone!

107   Sweet friends, in joy assembled here together,   110   75
      Never forget us, once your sweetest friends.
      Before you greet the jug, Khayaam adjures you:
      When his turn comes, turn down his empty bowl.

108   Khayaam, who stitched the hides for Wisdom's tent
      Has tumbled in Grief's clutches. He lies burning;
      The shears of Death have closed upon his guys
      And Hope the Broker sells him for a song.

109   Fools, with damnation as your destiny,
      Sentenced to fuel the eternal fires of Hell,
      How long will you still plead for Omar's pardon,
      Nudging his mercy from the Merciful?

110   Though pearls in praise of God I never strung,
      Though dust of sin lies clotted on my brow,
      Yet will I not despair of mercy. When
      Did Omar argue that the One was Two?

111   The palace with huge walls soaring to Heaven,   20
      Where prostrate Kings did reverence at the gate—
      A ring-dove perches on its battlements;
      'Where, where?' it coos, 'where, where?'

NOTES

The *abjad* system is one which gives letters of the alphabet
numerical meaning. Hence a number of mystical value
can be translated into a word, and vice-versa. 'Squanderer of
goods' in Sufi terminology is one who gives away or ignores
worldly goods which burden him in his voyage along the Sufi
path.

VERSE

1   According to some manuscripts a stone is flung into the
     cup as a signal for movement, but the better text has
     the cup filled with wine.

2   Fitzgerald's corresponding quatrain is borrowed from
     Hafiz's seventh ode.

5   The text here contains no reference to New Year's Day,
     as some commentators suppose. 'Live heart' is a Sufic
     technical term.

7   Fitzgerald's seventh quatrain is borrowed from Attar's
     Mantiq Taiyur.

8   Fitzgerald substitutes Nishapur for Balkh and Baghdad.

9   Jamshed was a king of the Kaianian dynasty.

10   Kawus and Kobad were kings of the Kaianian dynasty.
     Rustum, son of Zal, was a hero of ancient Persia;
     Hatim Tai, a famous philanthropist of mediaeval
     Arabia; and Tus, the one-time capital of Imperial
     Persia.

11/12 These two verses are telescoped in Fitzgerald's *A Book of Verses* quatrain.

13 Some versions have 'brother' in the last line. This is an obvious error; no poet of Khayaam's standing could have used, in a poem of such lofty diction, a form of address occurring only in bazaar greetings.

15 *Shabikhun* is here rendered 'ambush', to accentuate the element of surprise in death's stroke. 'Night attack', found in some translations, is incorrect.

17 Bahram, surnamed *Gur* because of his fondness for hunting the *Gur* or wild ass (*onager* in the Latin Vulgate), was a Sassanian king of Persia.

18 There is play here on the words *Gur*, 'wild ass' and *Gor*, 'the grave'.

21 The seven thousand years refer to the mythical age of the world. Translations which omit this number dull the point.

25 The Way is the *Tariqa* or path of the mystic; the Sufi technical term *munadi* must therefore be rendered 'guide', not 'proclamation' as in some versions, if the sense is to be preserved.

26 Professor Arberry suggests that the verse originally read *rufta* or 'sweep', rather than *rafta* or 'gone', in order to rhyme with *khufta* in the second line. This is not indicated by the original, and Persian poetic usage permits assonances of this sort.

29 The flight of the essential being in search of enlightenment is likened, in Sufic terminology, to that of a falcon.

32   This is the original of the verse which provoked
      Fitzgerald's famous 'blasphemous' quatrain.

38   Here Khayaam uses the phrase *zabani hal* or 'mystic
      tongue'. Western commentators have insisted on being
      puzzled by it.

39   Part of this verse went into Fitzgerald's quatrain 38; he
      combines it with a borrowing from Attar's *Mantiq*.

40   'Vision' refers to spiritual insight.

46   One translator has 'for the turn comes with a bellow'
      confusing *bukhur* ('drink') with *bakhaur* ('bellow').
      (*Romance of the Rubaiyyat*.)

54   The letter A, or *Alif*, stands for God. Thus Hafiz
      writes: 'He who knows One knows all'. And Jesus is
      said in the *Gospel of Thomas* to have told his teacher
      Zacchaeus: 'If thou knowest not *Alpha* according to its
      nature, how canst thou teach others the *Beta*?'

62   Here the Sufi technical terms *Zahir* and *Batin* are used
      for 'Esoteric' and 'Exoteric'; and *masti*, 'drunkenness', is
      allegorical of ecstasy.

64   Fitzgerald's 'angel shape' comes from his mis-reading
      of *piri* ('old man') for *pari* ('fairy'). Professor Arberry
      quotes this verse as one more evidence of Khayaam's
      'blasphemy', no trace of which, however, can be found
      in the original.

65   According to early tradition, Islam will one day be
      divided into seventy-two sects. Fitzgerald, in his
      Introduction, writes of the seventy-two 'religions'
      supposed to divide the world.

71   'Jihun' or 'Ilagird' is the Oxus.

74   This is the verse about which Fitzgerald wrote to
        Professor Cowell: 'I think that *u danad* must be some
        technical call at the *chaugan* (polo) game.'
        Arberry comments (*Romance of the Rubaiyyat*,
        1959): 'But did not Omar rather intend by the repeated
        ictus of '*u*' to imitate the repeated blow of the stick
        hitting the ball?' My own opinion is that Omar simply
        used *u danad*, 'He knows', to mean 'He knows' as any
        other literate Persian poet might have done.

89   This is the original of Fitzgerald's gratuitous attack on
        the Sufis with 'Sufi pipkin' etc.

90   Fitzgerald makes Omar call Ramazan the 'sullen
        month', an impiety which was not Omar's. Shaban
        immediately precedes Ramazan, the sacred month of
        fasting.

97   Professor Arberry (*Romance of the Rubaiyyat*) makes a
        surprising comment on this verse. He claims that the
        words *pusht pusht* in the last line have always puzzled
        readers. But *pusht* means 'back' and any literate Persian
        could have told him that *pusht pusht* means 'one after
        another', and that singular and plural are often inter-
        changed in poems to assist the metre. Arberry's novel
        explanation comes oddly from a scholar of his
        eminence. He claims that since 'porter' is singular
        pusht pusht must refer to the 'sole porter'. So he
        would have us amend the line by reading '*pusht bast*'
        ('load') which involves the mere elimination of one or

two embarrassing diacritical points, whereupon every-
thing 'becomes delightfully clear'. Yet to my certain
knowledge, no scribe has here written anything but
pusht pusht and a Persian-speaking scribe might
surely be allowed to know what he is copying out.

110 Khayaam uses the phrase *gauhar suftan*, 'to thread
pearls', in the poetic sense of stringing verses together.
Fitzgerald has missed the meaning of the One and Two,
thus destroying the sense of this most important
verse.

TWO COMPARATIVE RENDERINGS

Persian text

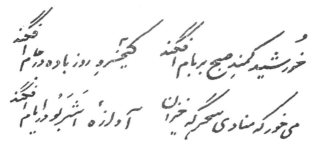

Romanized Persian text

Khurshid kamāndi sobh bar bām afgand

Kai Khusro i roz bādah dar jām afgand

Mai khur ki manad sahr ga khizān

Awaza i ishrabu dar ayām afgand.

Fitzgerald translation

Awake! for Morning in the Bowl of Night

Has flung the Stone that puts the Stars to flight:

And lo! the Hunter of the East has caught

The Sultan's Turret in a Noose of Light.

Graves–Shah translation

While Dawn, Day's herald straddling the whole sky,

Offers the drowsy world a toast 'To Wine',

The Sun spills early gold on city roofs—

Day's regal Host, replenishing his jug.

Persian text

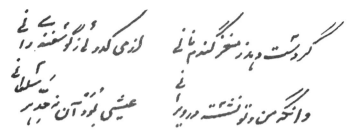

Romanized Persian text

Gar dast dihad zi maghzi gandum nāni
Az mai kaduī zi gusfandi rāni
Wa āngah man wa tu nishasta dar wairani
'Aish buwad ān na haddi har sultāni

Fitzgerald translation

A Book of Verses underneath the Bough,
A Jug of Wine, a Loaf of Bread, and Thou
Beside me singing in the Wilderness—
Ah, Wilderness were Paradise enow!

Graves–Shah translation

Should our day's portion be one mancel loaf,
A haunch of mutton and a gourd of wine
Set for us two alone on the wide plain,
No Sultan's bounty could evoke such joy.

Manuscripts of the Rubaiyyat

Royal Asiatic Society of Bengal. N.L. 160
Calcutta Madrassa Library. 14, 19/1
Bodleian Library, Oxford. (Ouseley MS)
Sultan Mhmd Nur. (Rosen II)
Berlin MS (Rosen I)
Tehran MS (Nicolas)
Lucknow Nawal Kishore MS (Whinfield)
Amritsar MS (Sheikh Ghulam Mhmd)
Khwaja Mhmd Salin MS
Mhmd bin Badri Jarjami MS
Professor Syed Najib Ashraf Nadvi MS
Bibliothèque Nationale MSS (Three MSS of Schefer Collection)
Gouri Prashad Saxena MS
Patna Oriental Public Library
Vienna MS
Uppsala MS
Istanbul MSS (Four)
St. Petersburg MS
Tonk MS (Library of the Nawab of Tonk)
Tehran MS II
Qasim Ghani MS
Qazvini MS
Syed Nafisi MS
Syed Jalaluddin Shemali MS
Ashrafuddin Malikzai MS
Papazai Foundation Library MS

[NOTE. *I have omitted from this list the A.D. 1259 MS in the Chester Beatty Library and the A.D. 1207 MS in the Cambridge University Library since some doubt has been expressed as to their authenticity.   O. A-S.*]

Collections containing Khayaam Verses

Mirsad ul Ibad, *Najm ul Din Razi.*
Tarikh i Jahan Gusha, *Juwayni.*
Nuhsat ul Arwah, *Shahrazuri.*
Tarikh i Guzida, *Hamidullah Mustawfi.*
Firdaws ul Tarikh.
Munis ul Ahrar.
Kulliyat, *Ibn al Yamin.*
Tarikh ul Herat, *Saiful Mhmd.*
Shahiran Tarika, *abu Said Khwajagani.*
Khulasat ul Ashaar wa Zubdat ul Afkar. *Taqi Kashani.*
Rahat us Sudur, *Rawandi.*
Marzuban Name, *Sadruddin Warwini.*
Risala i Qalandariyya, *abu Ishaq*
Falak wa Falakat, *abu Wais Perishani.*

GENERAL BIBLIOGRAPHY

Mir Khond, *History of the Assassins.*
Khondemir, *Habib us Siyar, Dabistan.*
Ibn Khalliqan, *Wafiat ul Ayan.*
Abu Faraj.
Abul Feda.
Ibn Khaldun, *Tarikh ul Imam.*
Shahrastani, *Milal wa Nihal.*
Shahrazuri, *Nuhsat ul Arwah.*
Ibn ul Athir.
Feriduddin Attar, *Mantiq, Tazkirat ul Awliah.*
Hafiz, *Diwan.*
Jami, *Yusuf wa Zuleikha, Nahfat ul Uns.*
Rumi, *Mathnavi.*
Nizami, *Chahar Maqala.*
Lutf Ali beg Adhar, *Atish Kedeh.*

Saadi, *Gulistan*.
Hujwiri, *Revelation of the Veiled*.
Shah I. *The Sufis*.
Hakim Sanai, *Walled Garden of Truth*.
Qutbuddin Papazai, *Israf Namah*.
Burhanuddin Papazai, *Iflas Namah*.
Al Ghazali, *Ihya ul Ulum*.
Al Tahanawi, *Kashaf Istilihat ul Funun*.
Abu Afifi. *Philosophy of Ibn ul Arabi*.
Aflaki, *Munaqib ul Arifin*.
Badawi, *Shahadat ul Ishq*.
Gardner, W. H. T., *Mishkat of Ghazali*.
Abu Mansur Hallaj, *Diwan*.
Ibn ul Arabi, *Fusus ul Hikam*.
Ibn Hanbal, *Mushad*.
Ibn Sina, *Kitab ul Najat*.
Shahbuddin Suhrawardi, *Kitab Hikmat ul Ishraq*.
Nizam ul Mulk, *Siasatnamah*.
Imam Zamakshari, *Tafsir ul Kawhaf*.
Imam Salahuddin Behaddi, *Kawakib min ul kawakib fi Kowkub*.
Ibn Qutaibah, *Al Shiv wa 'l Shuara. Kiteb al Maarif*.